Monstrous Morgues
of the Past

by Dinah Williams

Consultant: Troy Taylor
President of the American Ghost Society

BEARPORT
PUBLISHING

New York, New York

Credits

Cover and Title Page, © Grischa Georgiew/Shutterstock, © Antonova Christina/Shutterstock, and © Anyka/Shutterstock; 4–5, © Muammer Mujdat Uzel/iStockphoto and Exactostock/SuperStock; 6, © Bettmann/Corbis; 7T, © Alysta/Shutterstock; 7B, © Siamionau Pavel/Shutterstock; 8, © Isaac Oboka; 9, © Corbis/SuperStock; 10, © The Granger Collection, New York; 11, © Arthur Schatz/Time Life Pictures/Getty Images; 12, © Bettmann/Corbis; 13, Courtesy of the Karl J. Sup Collection, Eastland Memorial Society; 14, Courtesy of Mark Wells; 15, Courtesy of Mark Wells; 16, © Colorado Coalition of Paranormal Investigators (CCPI); 17T, © Tomek Sikora/The Image Bank/Getty Images; 17B, © Colorado Coalition of Paranormal Investigators (CCPI); 18, © April A. Taylor Photography; 19, © Elzbieta Sekowska/Shutterstock; 20, Courtesy of The Memphis Convention and Visitors Bureau; 21, © Steve Cox; 22, © DigitalVues/Alamy; 23L, © 1886 Crescent Hotel; 23R, Courtesy of Anthony Silva; 24, © Francis Miller/Time Life Pictures/Getty Images; 25T, San Luis Obispo County Telegram-Tribune 10-30-1960 © The Tribune; 25B, © AP Images; 26, © AP Images/Jessica Hill; 27T, © Olmar/Shutterstock; 27B, © Lions Gate/Courtesy Everett Collection; 31, © D. Russell 78/Shutterstock.

Publisher: Kenn Goin
Editorial Director: Adam Siegel
Creative Director: Spencer Brinker
Design: Dawn Beard Creative
Cover: Kim Jones
Photo Researcher: Omni-Photo Communications, Inc.

Library of Congress Cataloging-in-Publication Data

Williams, Dinah.
  Monstrous morgues of the past / by Dinah Williams.
     p. cm. — (Scary places)
  Includes bibliographical references (p.   ) and index.
  ISBN-13: 978-1-61772-149-6 (library binding)
  ISBN-10: 1-61772-149-2 (library binding)
  1. Haunted morgues—Juvenile literature. 2. Ghosts—Juvenile literature. I. Title.
  BF1476.4.W55 2011
   133.1'22—dc22

                              2010036464

For more information, write to Bearport Publishing Company, Inc., 101 Fifth Avenue, Suite 6R, New York, New York 10003. Printed in the United States of America in North Mankato, Minnesota.

122010
10810CGF

10 9 8 7 6 5 4 3 2 1

Contents

Imagine dead bodies lying in the cold darkness. They silently wait to be placed in their final resting place—the **grave**. No wonder people are terrified by **morgues**. Death and decay are everywhere in these buildings—which shouldn't come as a surprise. After all, morgues are places where people prepare dead bodies for **funerals** or perform **autopsies** to find out the cause of a person's death.

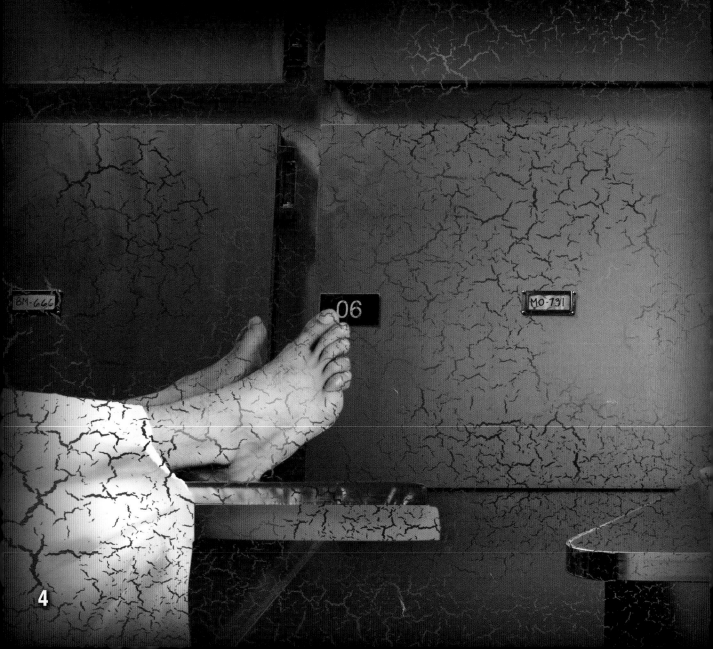

Morgues can be found in hospitals, **funeral homes**, and **mortuaries**. They are places where many people say they have seen the **spirits** of dead bodies lurking in the shadows. Among the 11 morgues in this book, you'll discover former funeral homes where the dead refuse to leave, a morgue that had more than one million visitors each year, and a haunted house that has a basement where people once drained the blood from dead bodies.

A View of Death

Paris Morgue, Paris, France

In the early 1800s, unidentified dead bodies in Paris were taken to the city's morgue. Family members or friends would come there, hopefully, to identify the **corpses** and agree to give them a proper burial. The building was open from dawn until dusk, seven days a week. What began as a place to identify bodies, however, soon became one of Paris's biggest tourist attractions.

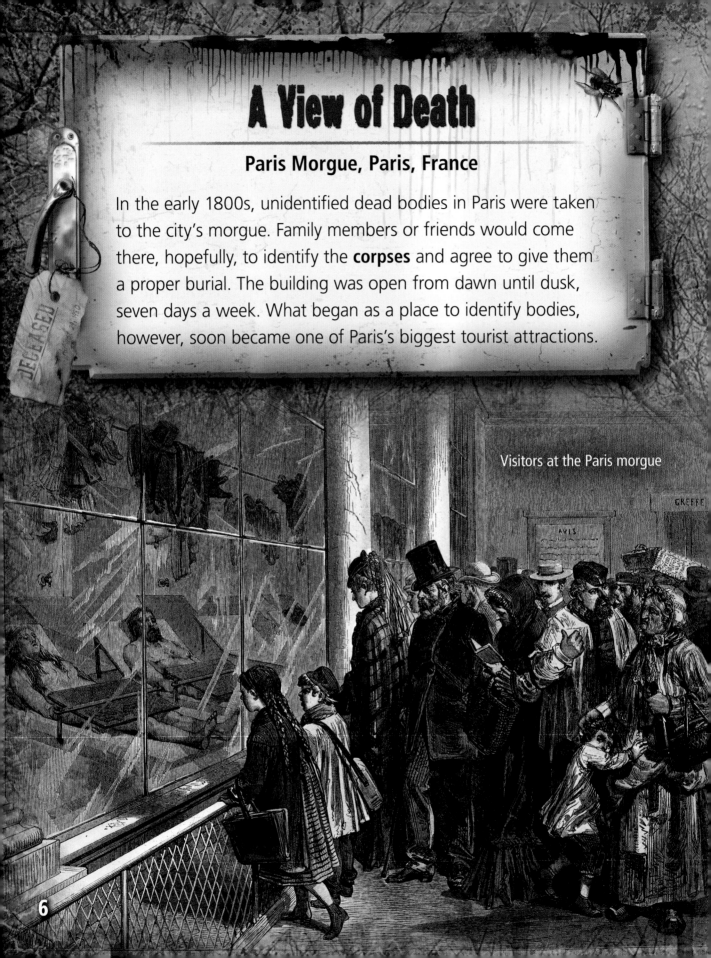

Visitors at the Paris morgue

Curious visitors crowded into the Paris morgue to look at the dead. As a result, a bigger morgue was built in 1864 near the Notre Dame **Cathedral**. Inside the new building was a large room with a glass wall. Behind the wall were 12 black marble tables lit by a skylight.

Notre Dame Cathedral

Unidentified bodies were displayed on the tables for as long as two weeks. Beside each corpse's head was a faucet so the workers at the morgue could sprinkle water and chemicals on the bodies to try to keep them from rotting. When refrigerators were invented, they were used to help preserve the bodies.

In November 1876, two packages containing the top and bottom of a woman's corpse were delivered to the morgue. The story of a woman cut to pieces caused a sensation. When put on display, her body was viewed by as many as 20,000 people in one day. Through police work, the woman's murderer was eventually caught—and put to death.

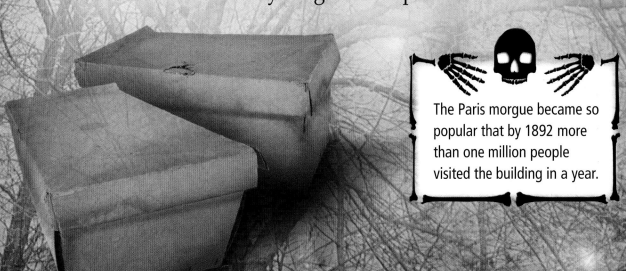

The Paris morgue became so popular that by 1892 more than one million people visited the building in a year.

Death by Ice Pick

The Morgue at St. Elizabeth's Hospital, Washington, D.C.

St. Elizabeth's Hospital was America's first **federal** mental institution. From 1855 to 2002, more than 125,000 patients were treated there. Unfortunately, many of them ended up dying at St. Elizabeth's as well. Thousands of their brains remained in the hospital's morgue long after their deaths.

The autopsy room at St. Elizabeth's Hospital

The morgue at St. Elizabeth's was always busy. Between 1884 and 1982, more than 15,000 autopsies were performed there. Doctors were looking for defects or injuries to the brain that might cause people to be **mentally ill**. As a result, they kept a collection of more than 1,400 brains in glass jars. The morgue also had 5,000 photographs of brains and 100,000 slides of patients' brain tissue.

One doctor at St. Elizabeth's, Walter Freeman, was especially interested in the relationship between the brain and mental illness. He performed a risky brain surgery called a **lobotomy**, which was supposed to lessen the **symptoms** of mentally ill patients. During the surgery, Dr. Freeman would hammer an ice pick through a patient's **eye sockets** in order to cut nerve connections in the brain. Dr. Freeman performed more than 3,000 lobotomies on patients during his career. Unfortunately, about 15 percent of those people died.

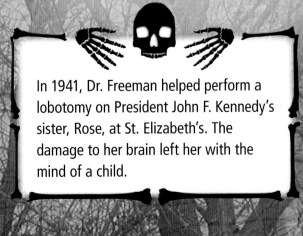

In 1941, Dr. Freeman helped perform a lobotomy on President John F. Kennedy's sister, Rose, at St. Elizabeth's. The damage to her brain left her with the mind of a child.

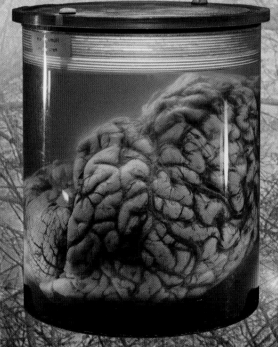

Forgotten at Potter's Field

Bellevue Hospital's Morgue, New York City

Bellevue Hospital's morgue opened in 1866 in New York City. During that first year, 105 bodies were taken there. Today, more than 20,000 bodies pass through the morgue each year. Many are eventually claimed by friends or family and are then given a proper burial. Yet what happens to the 8,500 bodies each year that are not claimed by anyone?

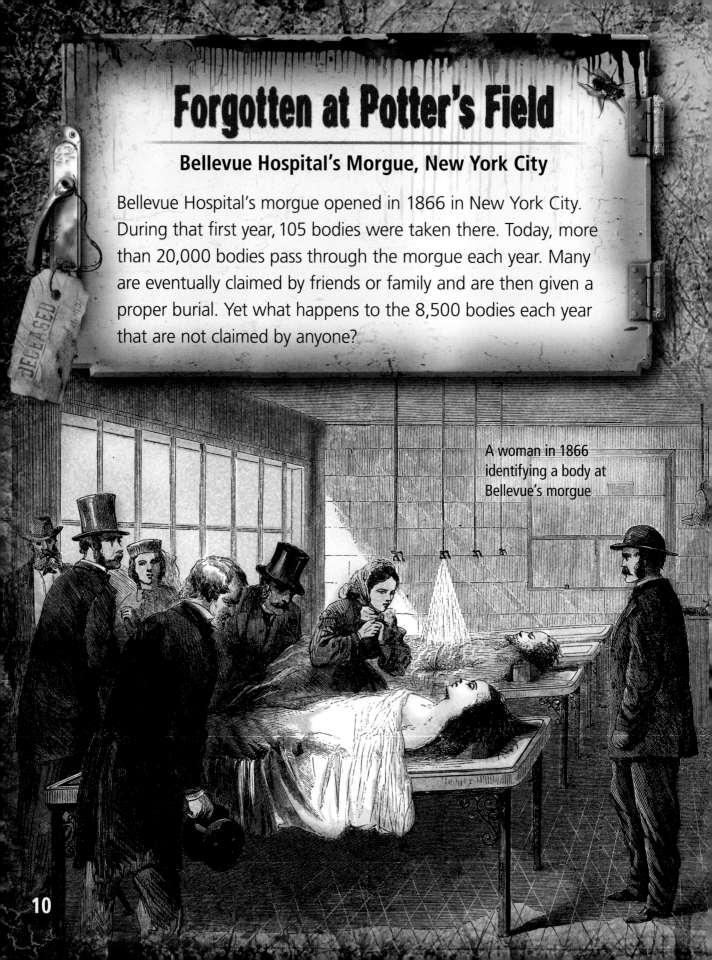

A woman in 1866 identifying a body at Bellevue's morgue

Each unidentified body that arrives at Bellevue's morgue is photographed and described. The information is sent to the police department's Bureau of Missing Persons to see if it matches the description of anyone in their records.

Corpses lie in refrigerated vaults at Bellevue for two or more weeks, awaiting identification. After that time, if they are still unclaimed, some of the **cadavers** are given to **embalming** schools, where students can practice preserving them. Other corpses are sent to medical schools so that students can cut them open and study their body parts. The remainder are buried in the New York City Cemetery, known as Potter's Field, on Hart Island. The cemetery was established in 1869 as a burial spot for people too poor to afford a funeral or for unclaimed bodies.

Angel Brito, who had worked for 14 years as a hospital officer at Bellevue, died in 2009. He had no family to claim him, so his body lay in the Bellevue morgue for two months. When his fellow officers found out, they raised $1,900 for a funeral. "We refused to let him go to Potter's Field," said a fellow coworker.

More than 750,000 people are buried in Potter's Field. Prisoners from the jail on nearby Rikers Island are paid to dig large graves. Each one holds 150 adult coffins. Between 2,000 and 3,000 bodies are buried on the island each year.

Prisoners burying bodies in Potter's Field

Drowned but Not Dead?

Temporary Morgue from the *Eastland* Disaster of 1915, Chicago, Illinois

On July 24, 1915, a steamship called the *Eastland* rolled over in the Chicago River. More than 800 passengers died. Some say that the **temporary** morgue that housed these victims is still haunted by their ghosts.

Victims of the *Eastland* disaster

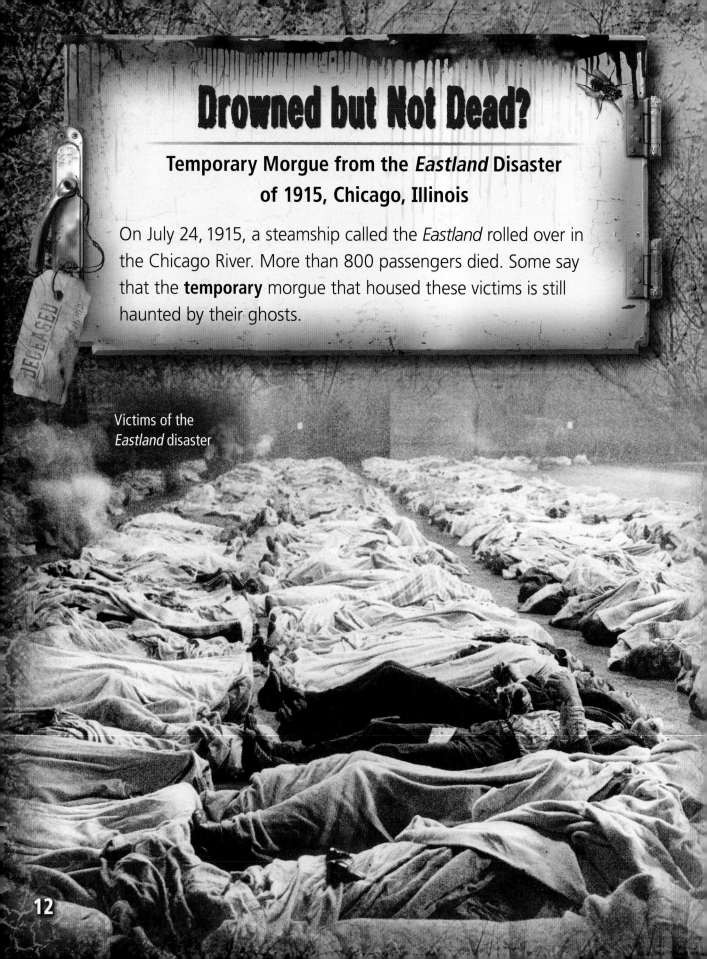

The *Eastland*, packed with more than 3,000 people, was bound for a picnic. While still tied to the **dock**, the poorly built ship toppled over. Passengers on the top **deck** were thrown into the water. Those below deck were trapped. Despite being only 20 feet (6 m) from shore, 841 passengers died, including 22 entire families.

The Second Regiment Armory, where military equipment was stored, became a temporary morgue to hundreds of corpses from the disaster. "Nearly every room on the lower floors of the warehouse contained bodies," reported a newspaper. "The remaining space was filled with crowds of policemen, rescuers, and friends and relatives of the dead." There were 50 embalmers on hand as well.

When TV host Oprah Winfrey established Harpo Studios in the Armory in 1989, workers quickly discovered the building was haunted. Security guards reported the spooky sounds of ghostly laughter and women sobbing. Others have seen a ghost called the "Gray Lady" floating down hallways. She wears a dress that looks like it is from 1915. Her image has even been caught on security cameras!

Charles "Reggie" Bowles, a 17-year-old volunteer diver, was nicknamed the Human Frog. He worked furiously the day of the *Eastland* wreck to bring victims to the surface. By nightfall, he had found 40 bodies.

The *Eastland* after it rolled onto its side

The Morgue in the Basement

Baxter Avenue Morgue, Louisville, Kentucky

In 1901, Victor Vanderdark opened the Vanderdark Funeral Home on Baxter Avenue. What began as a respectable business soon became a place of nightmares.

According to stories people told, Victor Vanderdark mysteriously left his family—and his business—in 1932. After Victor's disappearance, control of the funeral home went to his only son, Warren. He was considered odd, and business slowed down. Within a few years, Warren's wife, Lily, also vanished mysteriously, along with their eight-year-old daughter, Diedra. Frightened by these strange disappearances, even fewer customers came to the funeral home.

To increase business, Warren changed the company's name to the Baxter Avenue Morgue. People still stayed away, however, and the morgue closed for good by 1940. Yet why was the light in the basement always on? What was Warren doing? Reports of missing people and pets from the neighborhood began to increase. In 1951, Warren disappeared as well.

For nearly 50 years, the morgue in the basement lay undisturbed. Ghost hunters, however, have seen lots of activity there, including chairs knocked over and spirits running down hallways. They have even recorded a young girl saying, "Daddy, why'd you do that?" Could it be the missing Diedra trying to tell a visitor something?

The Baxter Avenue Morgue is now home to one of America's scariest haunted houses.

Hospital Haunting

Hotel Colorado, Glenwood Springs, Colorado

The Hotel Colorado opened in 1893. For more than 100 years, guests at this **luxurious** hotel have included everyone from presidents to **gangsters**. While serving as a temporary naval hospital during World War II (1939–1945), however, some of its patients became permanent residents.

The Hotel Colorado

So many U.S. soldiers were injured during World War II that hospitals didn't have enough room to care for them all. To help out, the Hotel Colorado was converted into a naval hospital in 1942. A morgue was created in the hotel's basement to store the bodies of patients who could not be saved. According to some, spirits of these dead soldiers still linger there. The current staff of the hotel has reported locked doors mysteriously opening and lights turning themselves off and on in this area.

The part of the hotel that served as a morgue isn't the only spooky part of the building. During the war, a maid was murdered in the Hotel Colorado. Some say her screams can still be heard echoing in the hallways. The room where she died has so much ghostly activity that the hotel does not rent it out to guests.

Some people claim that the ghost of a woman has been seen watching over some of the hotel's male guests as they sleep. Perhaps she is a nurse from the hospital trying to make sure her patients don't end up in the morgue.

This hallway in the hotel's basement leads to the area that once served as a morgue.

New Orleans Ghosts

The Mortuary, New Orleans, Louisiana

PJ McMahon and Sons was one of the most beautiful funeral homes in New Orleans. More than 20,000 funerals were held there over 70 years. Yet time and a hurricane made sure nothing remained but the ghosts.

The Mortuary

In 1872, Mary Slattery built a gorgeous mansion in New Orleans for her large family. They lived there for more than 30 years. In the 1920s, PJ McMahon bought the building. He made it into a luxurious funeral home, with autopsy and embalming rooms, as well as a **crematorium**.

The business was incredibly successful until it became too expensive to run and was forced to close down in 2004. Then, in 2005, the building was severely damaged by Hurricane Katrina. Yet two years later, a company bought the abandoned morgue and turned it into a popular haunted house during the Halloween season. They also gave the old morgue a new name—the Mortuary.

What the company didn't count on, however, is that the building seems to be actually haunted. Customers at the haunted house say they have been poked and pushed by phantom fingers. The spirits of two children, thought to be those of Mary Slattery, like to play pranks on visitors. In addition, workers claim to have seen a long-dead **mortician** doing his bloody work in the autopsy room.

More than 30 cameras and microphones have been placed throughout the Mortuary to record its ghostly activity.

From Morgue to Museum

National Ornamental Metal Museum, Memphis, Tennessee

In 1979, a group of buildings in Memphis was turned into the National Ornamental Metal Museum. More than 100 years earlier, however, the buildings had served a different purpose. They had been part of the U.S. **Marine** Hospital. During the **yellow fever epidemic** of 1878, hundreds of bodies passed through the hospital's morgue. Maybe that is why some say spirits still visit the museum.

The basement of this building was once used as the morgue for the U.S. Marine Hospital.

Yellow fever, a disease spread by mosquitoes, had always plagued Memphis. Yet nothing prepared the city for the epidemic of 1878. On August 13, the first death was reported. By the middle of October, about 17,000 people were infected and 5,150 were dead.

Many of the sick were treated at the U.S. Marine Hospital, which was made up of houses for doctors, nurses, and officers, as well as the hospital itself. The doctor's house had a small morgue in the basement. Doctors used a chute to send dead bodies from the main floor of the building to the morgue. It served almost as a gateway between the living and the dead.

Recently, ghost hunters have heard mysterious whispers in the part of the museum that was once the morgue. They have also seen unexplained dark shapes moving down the hall. Some museum workers claim they have been visited by a ghostly man in a wheelchair. He was seen roaming the second floor of the doctor's house in the 1980s. When the rooms were repainted, however, he never appeared again. Perhaps he didn't like the new color.

When the hospital's buildings were being renovated to turn them into a museum, one worker got a surprise. She claimed that when she looked through a hole in the ceiling she saw a ghost's face peering back down at her.

Doctors slid bodies down this chute to send them to the morgue below.

Doctor of Death

1886 Crescent Hotel & Spa, Eureka Springs, Arkansas

The 1886 Crescent Hotel & Spa is a luxurious hotel. It was built near the **springs** of Eureka, which were thought to heal everything from kidney troubles to asthma. When the hotel fell on hard times in the 1930s, it was turned into a **cancer** center by a man claiming to be a doctor. If his patients survived the deadly disease, it certainly wasn't because of his phony cures.

The 1886 Crescent Hotel & Spa

In 1937, Norman Baker was in trouble in Iowa for pretending to be a doctor. So he moved to Arkansas, where he opened a cancer center in the former Crescent Hotel. He claimed he could cure the disease in a matter of weeks.

Some patients were treated with a liquid that included tea made from watermelon seeds, brown corn silk, and clover leaves. The mixture didn't cure anyone—and many of Baker's patients ended up in the building's morgue. In 1939, Baker was finally arrested for using his fake medical treatments. He was sent to prison in Kansas, and the cancer center was closed.

Baker's morgue, however, still exists on the lower levels of the hotel, complete with his autopsy table. It was here that Baker was said to cut apart bodies, trying to find a cure for cancer. Recently, ghost hunters have recorded an image of a lost soul who haunts the morgue. Other sightings in the hotel include Baker, dressed in the purple tie and white suit that he often wore.

Norman Baker

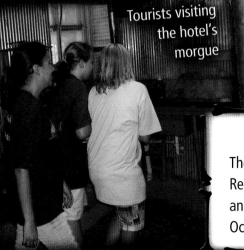

Tourists visiting the hotel's morgue

The 1886 Crescent Hotel & Spa reopened in 1946. Recently, it offered brave guests the chance to spend an overnight stay in the morgue during the month of October—the perfect way to celebrate Halloween.

A Deadly Crash

Alvin W. Walker Mortuary, Toledo, Ohio

In 1933, Alvin Walker opened a large funeral home in Toledo. For decades, he helped the people of Ohio bury their loved ones. He led a quiet life until a plane dropped from the sky.

This plane, carrying the California Polytechnic State University football team, crashed in Toledo, Ohio.

On October 29, 1960, the fog was so thick by midnight that it was hard to see the runway of the Toledo Express Airport. Yet a plane carrying the California Polytechnic State University football team took off anyway. Less than 300 feet (91 m) in the air, the left engine gave out, and the plane crashed in an orchard. Twenty-two people were killed.

According to one of the players who survived, the lifeless bodies were wrapped in blankets and stacked up at the small airport. Many of them were quickly taken to Walker Mortuary. That night, all alone, the mortuary owner's wife said she heard one of the dead players get up and walk around. Terrified, she called her husband and begged him to come home. He said he was too busy helping ambulances bring victims to the hospital, however. According to some, the football players' ghosts continued to roam around in the morgue for many years following their deaths.

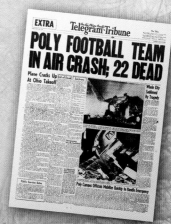

The plane crash made headlines in newspapers.

Years after the plane crash, the morgue was shut down and abandoned. Yet people said they still saw a light on in the upper floor. They also reported that a young woman in a dress would come to the window. After a few appearances, the police came to investigate. When they got to the top floor, they found nothing but a layer of undisturbed dust.

A memorial service was held for the football players who died.

The Haunting in Connecticut

Hallahan Funeral Home, Southington, Connecticut

The Hallahan Funeral Home opened in a charming house in 1936. Fifty years later, the business had moved to another location, and the building was rented out so that a family could live in it. That is when the hauntings began.

The Hallahan Funeral Home

In 1986, the Snedeker family moved into what they thought was a beautiful home. When they explored the basement, however, they found a box of coffin handles and a blood drainage pit used to prepare bodies for embalming. That's when they learned they were living in a former funeral home—with a basement that had been used as a morgue!

After settling into the house, the family began experiencing strange **phenomena**. They heard the sounds of hundreds of birds taking flight and saw strange people who suddenly disappeared. Clear water would turn a bloody red when it was used to mop the floor. The family also claimed to smell rotting flesh and decay throughout the house.

The family brought **paranormal researchers** to the house. The researchers lived there for a number of weeks and experienced the same phenomena as the Snedekers. To put an end to the creepy events, the homeowners called in a priest who helped rid the house of its evil spirits.

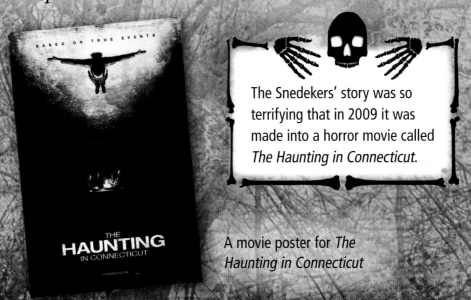

The Snedekers' story was so terrifying that in 2009 it was made into a horror movie called *The Haunting in Connecticut*.

A movie poster for *The Haunting in Connecticut*

Alvin W. Walker Mortuary
Toledo, Ohio

A deadly plane crash leads to a ghostly morgue.

Temporary Morgue from the *Eastland* Disaster of 1915
Chicago, Illinois

A ship topples over and turns an armory into a morgue.

Hotel Colorado
Glenwood Springs, Colorado

A hotel becomes a hospital and a home to ghosts.

1886 Crescent Hotel & Spa
Eureka Springs, Arkansas

A fake doctor and his "cures" are said to result in some real ghosts.

National Ornamental Metal Museum
Memphis, Tennessee

Spirits of yellow fever victims still linger at this former hospital.

NORTH AMERICA

Hallahan Funeral Home
Southington, Connecticut

A morgue becomes a haunted home.

Bellevue Hospital's Morgue
New York City

Thousands of unclaimed bodies end up in Potter's Field.

The Morgue at St. Elizabeth's Hospital
Washington, D.C.

Brains were stored in this mental hospital morgue.

Baxter Avenue Morgue
Louisville, Kentucky

Warren Vanderdark left behind a mysterious basement morgue.

SOUTH AMERICA

Pacific Ocean

The Mortuary
New Orleans, Louisiana

This Halloween haunted house is truly haunted.

Around the World

Arctic
Ocean

Paris Morgue
Paris, France
_____
A million visitors a year
viewed the unidentified dead.

EUROPE

ASIA

AFRICA

Indian
Ocean

Atlantic
Ocean

AUSTRALIA

Southern
Ocean

ANTARCTICA

Glossary

autopsies (AW-top-seez) examinations of dead people that are used to find out the cause and time of death

cadavers (kuh-DAV-urz) dead bodies of people

cancer (KAN-sur) a serious, often deadly disease

cathedral (kuh-THEE-druhl) a large, important church

corpses (KORPS-iz) dead bodies

crematorium (*kree*-muh-TOR-ee-uhm) a place where dead bodies are burned to ash

deck (DEK) the floor of a ship or boat

dock (DOK) a landing area where ships load and unload goods

embalming (im-BAHLM-ing) treating a dead body to prevent decay

epidemic (*ep*-uh-DEM-ik) a disease that spreads quickly

eye sockets (EYE SOK-its) bony holes in the skull that surround and protect the eyeballs

federal (FED-ur-uhl) having to do with the government of a nation

funeral homes (FYOO-nuh-ruhl HOHMZ) places where dead bodies are prepared for burial or cremation, and where funerals are held

funerals (FYOO-nuh-ruhlz) ceremonies that are held after a person dies

gangsters (GANG-sturz) people who are part of a group of criminals

grave (GRAYV) a hole dug into the ground where a dead person is buried

lobotomy (loh-BOT-uh-mee) a surgical procedure meant to calm violent people; a sharp instrument is forced into the brain through the eye socket in order to cut some of the nerve connections in the patient's brain

luxurious (lug-ZHOOR-ee-uhss) fancy and comfortable

Marine (muh-REEN) having to do with a branch of the U.S. military; Marines are trained to fight on both land and sea

mentally ill (MEN-tuhl-ee IL) having a mind that is not working normally

morgues (MORGZ) places where dead bodies are kept before being buried

mortician (mor-TI-shuhn) a person who prepares a body for a funeral

mortuaries (MOR-choo-*air*-eez) places where dead bodies are kept before being buried

paranormal researchers (*pa*-ruh-NOR-muhl REE-sur-churz) people who study events or collect information about things that cannot be scientifically explained

phenomena (fuh-NOM-uh-nuh) occurrences that one can sense

spirits (SPIHR-its) supernatural creatures, such as ghosts

springs (SPRINGZ) sources of water that flow from the ground

symptoms (SIMP-tuhmz) signs of a disease or other physical problems felt by a person

temporary (TEM-puh-*rair*-ee) lasting for a short period of time; not permanent

yellow fever (YEL-oh FEE-vur) a deadly disease caused by a virus that is spread through the bite of a mosquito

Bibliography

Roach, Mary. *Stiff: The Curious Lives of Human Cadavers.* New York: W. W. Norton & Company (2003).

Schwartz, Vanessa R. *Spectacular Realities.* Berkeley, CA: University of California Press (1998).

Read More

Hamilton, John. *Haunted Places.* Edina, MN: ABDO Publishing Company (2007).

Joyce, Jaime. *Toe Tagged: True Stories from the Morgue.* New York: Franklin Watts (2007).

Stair, Nancy L. *Choosing a Career in Mortuary Science and the Funeral Industry.* New York: Rosen (2002).

Learn More Online

To learn more about morgues, visit
www.bearportpublishing.com/ScaryPlaces

Index

About the Author

Dinah Williams is an editor and children's book author. Her books include *Shocking Seafood*; *Slithery, Slimy, Scaly Treats*; *Abandoned Insane Asylums*; *Haunted Houses*; and *Spooky Cemeteries*, which won the 2009 Children's Choice Book Award. She lives in Cranford, New Jersey.